Wacky Museums and Roadside Sights

Charlotte Luongo

STECK-VAUGHN

Harcourt Supplemental Publishers

www.steck-vaughn.com

Photography: Cover-a ©Harrod Blank/www.artcaragency.com; cover-b ©Dave G. Houser/CORBIS; p.3b-c ©Leila Cohoon/Leila's Hair Museum; p.4 ©David Garth/San Luis Obispo Chamber of Commerce; p.5a Courtesy of The Museum of Dirt; p.7 ©Gibson Stock Photography; p.9a Courtesy of Mildred O'Neill/The Shoe House; p.11 ©Philip James Corwin/CORBIS; p.13a Courtesy of Dog Bark Park; p.14 ©Gene L. O'Bryan/Courtesy of the Virginia (MN) Economic Development Authority; p.16 ©Peter Essick/Aurora; p.17b Courtesy of the Mt. Horeb Mustard Museum; p.18a ©Harrod Blank/www.artcaragency.com; p.19b ©Getty Images/Hulton Archive; p.20 ©Gibson Stock Photography; p.21b ©Andy Barker/Love Valley Shoppes, Inc.; p.22b ©Bettmann/CORBIS.

Additional Photography by Getty Royalty Free, PictureQuest, and the Steck-Vaughn Collection.

ISBN 0-7398-7518-3

Printed in China.

1 2 3 4 5 6 7 8 9 M 07 06 05 04 03

Contents

it's a
Wacky World!

STEP RIGHT UP!

Come visit a wild world where **wacky** is interesting. This world can be found along the roads of the United States.

That's right! You don't have to go too far to find **museums** and **attractions** that are run by people who see the world in a different way. These places might help you see the world in a different way, too.

Do you have your seat belt on? Let's begin at number one on the map of the United States.

1. World's Largest Ball of Twine, Cawker City, KS
2. Hair Museum, Independence, MO
3. Bubble Gum Alley, San Luis Obispo, CA
4. Museum of Dirt, Boston, MA
5. The House on the Rock, Spring Green, WI
6. The Corn Palace, Mitchell, SD
7. The Shoe House, Webster, SD
8. Prehistoric Gardens, Port Orford, OR
9. The Cockroach Hall of Fame, Plano, TX
10. Dog Bark Park, Cottonwood, ID
11. The World's Largest Floating Loon, Virginia, MN
12. The International Banana Club, Altadena, CA
13. Mount Horeb Mustard Museum, Mount Horeb, WI
14. International Hamburger Hall of Fame, Daytona Beach, FL
15. London Bridge, Lake Havasu, AZ
16. Love Valley, NC
17. Graceland, Memphis, TN

① WORLD'S LARGEST BALL OF TWINE

What is 40 feet around and **weighs** 17,320 pounds? It's the world's largest ball of **twine,** of course! The town of Cawker City, Kansas, proudly owns more than 6,938,709 feet of twine rolled up into one very big ball. That's almost long enough to reach across the state of Kansas three times!

Farmer Frank Stoeber had heard about a huge ball of twine in Darwin, Minnesota. In 1953, Stoeber decided to build his own **monument** to twine. Year after year he added more twine.

Sadly, when Stoeber died in 1974 his ball of twine was still smaller than the ball in Darwin. Hope was not lost, though. The people of Cawker City started adding to Stoeber's ball of twine. Each year the people of the city come together for a twine-adding picnic. Because of this, the world's largest ball of twine just keeps on growing and growing!

2 HAIR MUSEUM

Leila Cohoon of Independence, Missouri, has always loved hair. That is why Cohoon chose a job working with hair. She teaches people how to cut hair, but her love of hair goes beyond cutting it. Cohoon has her own hair museum.

The Hair Museum has more than two thousand pictures, rings, and other things all made from hair. The museum has hair that is more than 250 years old. Whatever kind or color of hair you want to see, there is a good chance that the Hair Museum will have it!

You might see these things at the hair museum. The woman in the picture is wearing something made from hair.

Many people have added their chewing gum to Bubble Gum Alley.

❸ BUBBLE GUM ALLEY

Yum, yum, **bubble gum!** If you like chewing great **gobs** of gum, then San Luis Obispo, California, is the place for you.

San Luis Obispo has a whole alley **devoted** to the greatest gob of bubble gum ever. Come to Bubble Gum Alley and add your own gum to the thousands of pieces of bubble gum stuck on the walls. Be careful, though. You don't want to get stuck yourself!

You'll find dirt of all colors at the Museum of Dirt.

④ MUSEUM OF DIRT

Most people don't think of Boston, Massachusetts, as the dirtiest city in America. Glenn Johanson is hard at work, though, trying to make it that way. Johanson runs Boston's Museum of Dirt.

The Museum of Dirt is devoted to dirt of all kinds. There is dirt from Mount Everest, Times Square, and the Panama Canal. There is dirt from Harry Truman's, Bob Hope's, and Elvis Presley's yards. You'll find dirt of every color there, from white to red to blue to pink.

Do you have your own bottle of interesting dirt? Feel free to add it to the museum's **collection.** You'll find it on the Web under *Museum of Dirt.*

CHAPTER 2

Buildings and Beyond

The wacky side of America can sometimes be seen in its buildings. Find out how walls and a roof can be turned into something more than just a building!

❺ THE HOUSE ON THE ROCK

If you could build your house anywhere in the world, where would you put it? Would you build it on top of a tall, thin rock? That is just what **architect** Alex Jordan did. He found a rock that was sixty feet tall in Spring Green, Wisconsin. Jordan decided that the rock would be the perfect place to live.

In the 1940s, Jordan started building his house by hand. He carried bags of stones to the top of the rock. As his house grew, people became interested in seeing the wacky home. Jordan had an idea. Why not turn the house into an attraction for **tourists?** Jordan began charging tourists to come inside his house.

The money helped Jordan make his house even bigger and wackier. One room in his house is made of glass. It took 3,264 pieces of glass to make the room's walls. The room hangs 218 feet off the side of the rock!

Jordan also filled his house with wild and wacky stuff. There is a giant sea monster, hundreds of music machines, and more strange attractions.

Here is a view of Jordan's glass room.

If you want to learn more about life in South Dakota, the Corn Palace is the place to go!

6 THE CORN PALACE

Corn is used in many ways. It is used to feed people and animals, but have you ever heard of corn being used to make a building? In Mitchell, South Dakota, there is a building that stands out from all the rest. It is covered from top to bottom in corn and other seeds! The building is called the Corn Palace.

The Corn Palace was built in 1921 by South Dakota farmers who wanted to show off their corn. Instead of painting the building, each year artists use corn, grass, straw, and seeds to cover the walls. The artists make pictures that show South Dakota life.

7 THE SHOE HOUSE

In Webster, South Dakota, there really is an old woman who lives in a shoe. She has so many boots and sneakers, she doesn't know what to do!

The woman's name is Mildred O'Neill. She moved to Webster in 1994. The town welcomed

Mildred O'Neill shows off some of the strange shoes she has collected.

her by building a giant shoe to house her collection. The giant shoe holds more than 7,000 shoes. The shoes **range** in size from tiny doll shoes to big clown shoes.

CHAPTER 3

Animal Attractions

If you like animals, this might be the chapter you'll love. Of course the animals you'll meet in these pages are not house pets. Move over puppies and kittens! Here come America's wacky animals!

🔴 8 PREHISTORIC GARDENS

Hidden in the rain forest of Port Orford, Oregon, is a **prehistoric** world. In it you will see **dinosaurs** peeking over treetops.

In the Prehistoric Gardens, more than twenty dinosaurs seem to run wild. A man named E.V. Nelson made these dinosaur **sculptures.** Before Nelson built his dinosaurs, he measured real dinosaur bones. Because he did that, the dinosaurs in the Prehistoric Gardens are the size of real dinosaurs.

The dinosaurs are painted in a range of bright yellows, oranges, and greens. The bright colors are fun to see, but the dark forest that **surrounds** the dinosaurs makes them seem real anyway.

This pair of dinosaurs seems to be at home in the Prehistoric Gardens' dark forest.

9 THE COCKROACH HALL OF FAME

Most people would be happy never to see a **cockroach.** Michael Bohdan of Plano, Texas, is different. Bohdan sees big brown bugs in a very wacky way. As a strange monument to his ugly six-legged friends, Bohdan started the wacky Cockroach Hall of Fame.

The Cockroach Hall of Fame houses art made from cockroaches. It also has some **famous** cockroaches. Pretty Marilyn Monroach has a bright red mouth. Liberoachi sits at a tiny piano wearing flashy clothes.

Many **visitors** to the Cockroach Hall of Fame think the wackiest things to see are the Madagascar hissing cockroaches. These cockroaches are three **inches** long! When you touch them, they hiss.

Madagascar hissing cockroaches are a big attraction at the Cockroach Hall of Fame.

This big dog welcomes visitors to Dog Bark Park.

⑩ DOG BARK PARK

Dennis Sullivan says that he can hear hundreds of dogs barking when he presses his ear to a piece of wood. Sullivan uses a saw to cut the dogs free from the wood. When he is finished cutting the wood, a sculpture of a dog is looking back at him.

Sullivan and his wife, Frances, have freed many wooden dogs in the same way. They keep their dogs at Dog Bark Park in Cottonwood, Idaho. Their largest sculpture is more than three stories tall! This huge dog sits at the front of the park. He doesn't bark, but he does give visitors a warm welcome.

Picture a school bus beside this loon to understand how big it is.

⑪ THE WORLD'S LARGEST FLOATING LOON

Loons are water birds that are often found in North America. In fact, the loon is the state bird of Minnesota. Virginia, Minnesota, might be the best loon town in the land.

Virginia is home to the World's Largest Floating Loon. This loon sculpture is almost as long as a school bus! It weighs 2,000 pounds. Even though it is so heavy, it floats on Silver Lake, just as a boat would.

This large loon cannot travel far across the water, though. A rope tied to the bottom of the lake keeps the bird in place.

Who doesn't like food? Some people are just crazy about certain kinds of food, though. This chapter is devoted to people who build monuments to their favorite food.

12 THE INTERNATIONAL BANANA CLUB

Some people get a **degree** in English or Spanish. Others get a degree in music. Some wacky people get a degree in **bananas.** The International Banana Club in Altadena, California, gives out these banana degrees.

An International Banana Club member with a big smile shows off items from the Banana Museum.

The International Banana Club has **members** from 27 different countries. These members have sent in more than 17,000 banana **items!** When a member sends in an item, he or she gets a banana point. Members who get many points get their banana degrees.

All of the International Banana Club's banana items are **displayed** at the Banana Museum. *The Guinness Book of Records* says the Banana Museum has the most items of one kind of fruit.

13 MOUNT HOREB MUSTARD MUSEUM

Wisconsin is known for its cheese. Anybody in Mount Horeb, Wisconsin, will tell you that Wisconsin should also be known for **mustard.** That's because Mount Horeb is home to the Mount Horeb Mustard Museum.

This museum has almost four thousand kinds of mustard! There is Dijon mustard, honey mustard, and even **chocolate-fudge** mustard. Now that's wacky!

If you like chocolate-fudge mustard, Mount Horeb, Wisconsin, is the place for you!

Harry Sperl shows off his hamburger bike.

🛑14 INTERNATIONAL HAMBURGER HALL OF FAME

What can you do with a **hamburger** besides eat it? Harry Sperl, also known as Hamburger Harry, sleeps in a hamburger bed. He rides to work on a hamburger bike. He often wears hamburger clothes. Of course, it is no surprise that Sperl also eats hamburgers every day.

Sperl owns the world's only hamburger museum, the International Hamburger Hall of Fame. The museum, **located** in Daytona Beach, Florida, is in Sperl's home. He is working with an architect to build his dream—a hamburger-shaped building to house his hamburger collection. ⚡

CHAPTER 5

A Blast from the Past

History comes to life along the roads of the United States of America. The wacky attractions in this chapter prove that not only is history still around, it can be strange and wonderful, too!

15 LONDON BRIDGE

Do you remember the song called London Bridge Is Falling Down? London Bridge really was falling down into the Thames River in London, England. That was before Robert McCulloch bought it for $2.5 million.

London Bridge once crossed the Thames River in London, England.

Now London Bridge crosses the Colorado River in Lake Havasu, Arizona.

McCulloch had big plans for his new bridge. The first thing he did was to take it apart. Then he sent the pieces of the bridge 10,000 miles from England to California. From there, the pieces went onto a truck. The truck carried the pieces all the way to the town of Lake Havasu in Arizona.

McCulloch had people from England help him put the bridge back together over the Colorado River. Now London Bridge is as strong as ever! ⚡

16 LOVE VALLEY

"Howdy! Welcome to the Wild West!" might be something you would hear when you entered the town of Love Valley, North Carolina. Of course, Love Valley is located nowhere near the real Wild West. That hasn't stopped its mayor, Andy Barker, from helping people **enjoy** the Wild West in North Carolina.

In Love Valley, you can kick up your boots and live the cowboy life. You won't find cars, TVs, or fast-food places in this town. Only cowboys, cowgirls, and horses live here.

You'll see only horses on the streets of Love Valley!

Graceland was the home of Elvis
Presley, the king of rock-and-roll.

🅘 GRACELAND

Elvis Presley was the
king of **rock-and-roll.**
Even though Elvis
died in 1977, people
still say that they
see the famous
star. People say
they have seen Elvis all
around the country.

Besides looking for Elvis or listening to
his rock-and-roll music, people visit his house,

Graceland. Every morning in Memphis, Tennessee, Graceland fills up with tourists. As they walk through the house, they look closely at each item on display.

Graceland is huge and full of wild attractions. You can walk through the Jungle Room with green floors. You can look at a bedroom with pink walls painted with dogs. Then there is the garage, where you can see Elvis's 22 cars and two airplanes!

LAST STOP ON YOUR WACKY ROAD TRIP

Now your road trip through the wacky side of America is coming to a close, but it is not over yet. There are wacky sights everywhere. Take a look at places that surround you. There is probably a cool attraction close by!

Remember to look at things in different ways. You just might find something that is very interesting!

GLOSSARY

architect (AHR kuh tehkt) *noun* An architect is a person who draws up plans for new buildings.

attractions (uh TRAK shuhnz) *noun* Places or things that people like to see are attractions.

bananas (buh NAN uhz) *noun* Bananas are long, yellow fruits.

bubble gum (BUHB uhl GUHM) *noun* Bubble gum is a kind of candy that you can chew but not eat.

chocolate-fudge (CHAWK luht FUHJ) *adjective* Something has a chocolate-fudge taste when it tastes like a candy made with milk, sugar, and ground cacao seeds.

cockroach (KAHK rohch) *noun* A cockroach is a large six-legged bug that is found all over the world.

collection (kuh LEK shuhn) *noun* A collection is a set of things that are alike in some way and that someone has saved.

degree (dih GREE) *noun* A degree is a paper that you get from a school. It says you have finished learning about something.

devoted (dih VOHT ihd) *adjective* Something that has been devoted to something else has been made or used only for that one thing.

dinosaurs (DY nuh sawrz) *noun* Dinosaurs were large animals that lived and died many, many years ago.

displayed (dih SPLAYD) *adjective* Something is displayed when it is put in a place where many people can see it.

enjoy (ehn JOY) *verb* To enjoy means to have a good time.

famous (FAY muhs) *adjective* To be famous is to be known by many people.

gobs (GAHBZ) *noun* Gobs are balls of something that is soft and sticky.

hamburger (HAM bur guhr) *noun* A hamburger is a sandwich made with cooked ground meat and a round bun.

history (HIHS tuh ree) *noun* History is anything that happened in the past and is written down somewhere.

inches (IHNCH ehz) *noun* Inches are used to measure something small.

items (YT uhmz) *noun* Items are things that you can see and touch.

located (LOH kayt ihd) *adjective* Something that is located in a place is found there.

loons (LOONZ) *noun* Loons are water birds that eat fish and live in lakes.

members (MEHM buhrz) *noun* Members are people who belong to something like a class or band.

monument (MAHN yoo muhnt) *noun* A monument is built to help people remember something or someone.

museums (myoo ZEE uhmz) *noun* Museums are places where things are stored and shown to people.

mustard (MUHS tuhrd) *noun* Mustard is a paste made from the seed of the mustard plant. People put it on food to make the food taste better.

prehistoric (pree hihs TAWR ihk) *adjective* A prehistoric time is a time before people wrote down things that happened.

range (RAYNJ) *verb* To range is to cover everything in a family of things.

rock-and-roll (RAHK and ROHL) *noun*
Rock-and-roll is a kind of music that people
have listened to from the 1950s to today. It has a
strong beat.

sculptures (SKUHLP chuhrz) *noun* Sculptures
are pieces of art that are not flat. They have been
shaped by fingers or other tools.

surrounds (suhr ROWNDZ) *verb* Surrounds
means lies all around a thing.

tourists (TUR ihsts) *noun* Tourists are people
who travel to a new place to see new sights and
have fun.

twine (TWYN) *noun* Twine is string often made
of dried grass.

visitors (VIHZ iht urhz) *noun* Visitors are
people who come to visit.

wacky (WAK ee) *adjective* To be wacky is to be
strange and funny.

weighs (WAYZ) *verb* When something weighs a
certain number of pounds, that tells how heavy
it is.

INDEX